Barbie™

Fun to Cook

A Dorling Kindersley Book

Dorling DK Kindersley

LONDON, NEW YORK, MUNICH, PARIS,
MELBOURNE, DELHI

Written and edited by Fiona Munro
Art Editor Goldy Broad
Art Director Cathy Tincknell
Publishing Manager Cynthia O'Neill
Associate Designers Jane Thomas, Laia Roses
Photography Dave King
Home Economist Katharine Ibbs
Production Nicola Torode
DTP Design Andrew O'Brien

Barbie photography by Tom Wolfson, Laura Lynch,
Mark Adams, Judy Tsuno and the
Mattel Photo Studio

First published in Great Britain in 2001 by
Dorling Kindersley Limited, 80 Strand, London WC2 ORL
A Penguin Company

6 8 10 9 7 5

ISBN 0-7513-2022-6

A CIP catalogue record for this book is available from
the British Library

Colour reproduction by Media Development
Printed and bound in China by Toppan

Dorling Kindersley would like to thank the following for
appearing in this book:
Polly Broad, Jake Davies, Jordan Davis, Alexandra Hayes,
Harriet Hunter, Jasmine Marsh, Nicola Mooi, Demi Ryan,
Jordann Sewell, Savina and Shirine Shah, Hannah Shone,
Shianne St Louis.

Dorling Kindersley would also like to
thank Kitschen Sync for loan of props.

see our complete
catalogue at
www.dk.com

Contents

Getting Ready to Cook!

I love cooking and it's easy when you know how! For each recipe inside, there are pictures of all the things you will need, from ingredients to kitchen tools as well as clear step-by-step guides to follow. Don't forget to ask an adult to help whenever you see the (!) symbol. Let's start!

Kitchen rules

It's important to follow these rules, every time you cook.

1 Be careful with sharp knives. Use a chopping board and keep fingers away from the blade.

2 Wear oven gloves to protect your hands if picking up hot things or using the oven or hob.

3 When you are using the hob, turn the saucepan handles to the side, so you do not knock them over.

4 When you take hot things out of the oven, put them on a wooden board, not straight onto the work surface.

5 Always wear an apron, tie back long hair, and wash your hands.

6 Read the recipe carefully and check that you have all the things you need.

7 Collect the ingredients you will need. Weigh and measure them out.

Tips on how to use this book:

If you are using the oven or grill, look here to find the temperature. Remember to turn on the oven or grill 20 minutes before you need them (preheating).

Words in *italic* type are explained more fully on page 48.

Look at this part of the page to find out how long the recipe will take to make.

Set the oven to 180°C/350°F/Gas Mark 4

20 minutes to make ♥ 15 minutes to bake ♥ LUNCHBOX IDEAS

Chunky Chocolate Cookies

If you really love chocolate then these cookies are just the treat for you! They are made with great big chunks of chocolate so they taste extra yummy. Take plenty to school in your lunchbox, because all your friends are sure to want one!

To make about 20 cookies you will need . . .

1 egg, beaten

100 g/4 oz softened butter

150 g/6 oz plain flour

75 g/3 oz soft light brown sugar

50 g/2 oz caster sugar

½ teaspoon salt

½ teaspoon bicarbonate of soda

150 g/6 oz good quality plain chocolate

½ teaspoon vanilla essence

Cook's tools

Chopping board

Baking sheet

Wire cooling rack

Wooden spoon

Palette knife

Scissors

Wax paper

Large mixing bowl

Plastic bag (like a freezer bag)

2 teaspoons

Rolling pin

Mmm, chocolate!

Great big chunks of chocolate!

1 Preheat the oven. Break chocolate into squares and put into plastic bag. Place on a solid surface.

2 With a rolling pin, break the chocolate into chunks. Keep your fingers out of the way!

3 In a bowl, *beat* butter with all the sugar until creamy and smooth. Gradually *beat* in egg.

4 *Beat* in flour, salt, vanilla, and bicarb of soda. Now stir in the chocolate chunks.

5 Spoon mounds onto a baking sheet lined with wax paper. Leave plenty of space around each one.

6 Bake for 10-15 minutes or until golden. Take out of the oven and leave for five minutes to harden, before moving to a wire rack to cool.

Barbie says: Try making these cookies with chunks of white or milk chocolate too!

16

17

Quantities for each recipe are shown in both metric and imperial measurements. Make sure you stick to using one set or the other, don't mix them up.

Each recipe includes a tip from Barbie. This might be a helpful hint or a suggestion on how to vary the taste or ingredients.

Look out for this symbol. It means you should ask an adult to help you with this part of the recipe.

A Fruity Feast

Here are two ideas for a fabulously fruity brunchtime treat, each using almost the same ingredients! Choose between a cool smoothie and a beautiful salad for a healthy, colourful kick-start to the day!

For a smoothie or a salad you will need . . .

100 ml/4 fl oz pineapple juice for a smoothie OR 2 tablespoons pineapple chunks for a salad.

8 large strawberries

1 ripe banana

1 tablespoon honey

3 tablespoons natural yogurt

Cook's tools

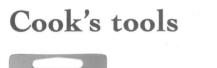

Chopping board

Large glass

Blender

Tablespoon

Sharp knife

1 To make a smoothie or a salad, first use a sharp knife to cut all the fruit up into chunks.

2 To make a salad, mix the yogurt with the honey, and layer with fruit in a glass. Serve.

1 To make a smoothie, put the fruit chunks, pineapple juice, yogurt, and honey into a blender. Put the lid on firmly.

2 Now *blend* until the mixture is smooth and pour into a large glass. Drink straight away!

Barbie says:
Try using other fruits like raspberries, blueberries, or mango!

Fresh, fruity fun!

You could decorate your salad with a tablespoon of muesli or nuts.

Sunshine Breakfast

Make this as a surprise for a special friend on her birthday, or on Mother's Day to show your mum how much you love her. It would make a lovely sunny surprise on a cold winter's day, too! Sometimes I just make it for myself though — I love to dip the toasty fingers into the creamy egg yolk. Mmm!

You will need . . .

2 slices of bread   ½ teaspoon butter   1 egg

Cook's tools

Large cookie cutter   Small bowl

Sharp knife

Chopping board

Non-stick frying pan   Ramekin   Fish slice

Barbie says:
When cooking your egg, keep the heat low so you don't burn the toast!

1 Use a bowl or saucer to cut a large circle from one slice of bread. With a cookie cutter, cut out a smaller circle inside.

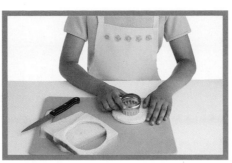

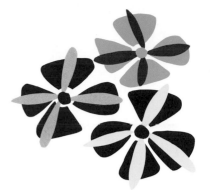

Sunny side up!

2 Remove crusts from second slice of bread and cut into fingers.

Make sure the hole you make in the bread is big enough for the egg!

3 Melt the butter in a frying pan over a low heat. Fry the bread, turning over when golden.

Lovely crunchy fingers – perfect for dipping!

4 Break the egg into a ramekin, then tip into hole in the bread. Fry gently until egg is cooked.

Mini Muffins

Everybody loves muffins!
Now you can impress your friends
and family by making delicious
fruity muffins yourself. They are so
easy and quick to make, soon you
will be experimenting with different
flavours! Muffins taste great eaten
warm from the oven, maybe with a
spoonful of sour cream.

To make about 20 you will need . . .

50 g/2 oz
butter

150 ml/
¼ pint milk

200 g/8 oz
plain flour

150 g/6 oz
caster sugar

2 teaspoons
baking powder

½ teaspoon
salt

1 egg, *beaten*

100 g/4 oz blueberries or raspberries

Cook's tools

Large mixing bowl   Saucepan   Sieve

Measuring
jug

Two
teaspoons

Wooden spoon   Paper cases

2 x 12 hole
muffin tins

Wire cooling rack

Barbie says:
When your muffins
are cooked, leave them
in the tin to cool down
a little so you don't
burn yourself!

1 Preheat the oven. Melt
butter in pan over a low
heat. Remove from hob
and stir in milk and egg.

2 *Sift* flour, baking
powder, and salt into
a mixing bowl. Stir in the
sugar and fruit.

3 Carefully add melted butter, milk, and egg mixture to the flour, sugar, and fruit mixture.

4 Now mix everything together quickly and gently. Don't worry if the mixture looks lumpy.

5 Using two teaspoons, transfer the mixture to muffin tins that you have lined with paper cases.

Yum, what fun!

6 Bake for about 20 minutes or until golden and well risen. Allow to cool in tin, then move to a wire rack.

Sandwich Stack

One of these fabulous sandwiches is just what you need in your lunchbox to keep you going during a busy day! As well as trying the ideas below, experiment with different breads such as rye or ciabatta. The fillings taste great on crackers, too!

You will need . . .

For a Turkey and Tomato Sub:

1 submarine roll

2 or 3 slices of turkey

3 slices of tomato

2 or 3 lettuce leaves

2 or 3 slices of cheese

1 tablespoon mayonnaise

For a Tuna Pitta Pocket:

1 pitta

1 teaspoon capers

2 tablespoons tinned kidney beans

3 tablespoons tinned tuna fish

1 tablespoon sweetcorn

For a Cream Cheese and Nut Bagel:

1 bagel

1 tablespoon raisins

1 apple, cored and *chopped*

1 tablespoon *chopped* nuts

2 tablespoons cream cheese

For a Mexican Wrap:

1 tortilla

6 to 8 strips of pepper (any)

1 tablespoon sour cream

2 or 3 lettuce leaves

1 teaspoon black or green olives, sliced

Cook's tools

Sharp knife

Table knife

Tablespoon

Teaspoon

Small mixing bowl

Cocktail sticks (optional)

Chopping board

Barbie says:
Knives can be dangerous. Ask an adult to help you cut bread.

Turkey and Tomato Sub

Spread the bottom of your sub with mayonnaise

Layer the lettuce, turkey, tomato, and cheese inside

Tuna Pitta Pocket

Mix all ingredients together and fill pocket!

Can't wait 'til lunch time!

Cream Cheese and Nut Bagel

Using a cocktail stick to hold your wrap together looks very stylish, but take it out before you start to eat!

Mexican Wrap

Layer lettuce, pepper, and olive slices along the middle of the flat tortilla

Mix all ingredients together and spoon onto bagel

Top with sour cream. Roll over one edge, then the other. Cut in half

Favourite Aprinana Cake

Apricots and bananas taste really great together! I like to bake this cake at the weekend and put slices in Skipper's lunchbox for her to share with friends at school. It's full of good things, and will fill you up until suppertime!

Barbie says:
Try using some *chopped* nuts or dried cranberries instead of apricots!

You will need . . .

100 g/4 oz softened butter

2 eggs, *beaten*

A little oil for greasing

200 g/8 oz plain flour

100 g/4 oz soft light brown sugar (plus 2 tblsps of demerara sugar for topping – optional)

Zest of ½ a lemon

1 teaspoon baking powder

½ teaspoon salt

50 g/2 oz dried apricots, *chopped*

3 ripe bananas, crushed

For the topping (optional):

Handful of dried banana slices

2 tablespoons honey

Cook's tools

1 kg/2 lb loaf tin

Wax paper

Scissors

Wire cooling rack

Chopping board

Sieve

Tablespoon

Large mixing bowl

Wooden spoon

Sharp knife

Grater

Brush

1 Preheat oven. Grease tin and line with a strip of wax paper the same width but twice the length of tin.

2 Put butter, sugar, and zest (see tip box on page 20) into a bowl and *beat* well. Gradually *beat* in eggs.

3 *Sift* the flour, baking powder, and salt into the mixture. *Beat* well. Stir in the apricots and bananas. Spoon into tin. Bake for one hour.

4 For topping: at the end of cooking time, spoon the honey over the cake and scatter over dried bananas. Sprinkle with demerara sugar and cook for another ten minutes.

5 Remove from oven and leave to cool in tin for ten minutes. Now, hold the ends of the paper, and move cake to wire rack until cold.

Chunky Chocolate Cookies

If you really love chocolate then these cookies are just the treat for you! They are made with great big chunks of chocolate so they taste extra yummy. Take plenty to school in your lunchbox, because all your friends are sure to want one!

To make about 20 cookies you will need . . .

1 egg, *beaten*

100 g/4 oz softened butter

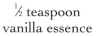

150 g/6 oz plain flour

75 g/3 oz soft light brown sugar

50 g/2 oz caster sugar

½ teaspoon salt

½ teaspoon bicarbonate of soda

150 g/6 oz good quality dark chocolate

½ teaspoon vanilla essence

Mmm, chocolate!

Cook's tools

Chopping board

Baking sheet

Wire cooling rack

Wooden spoon

Palette knife

Scissors

Wax paper

Rolling pin

Large mixing bowl

Plastic bag (like a freezer bag)

2 teaspoons

1 Preheat the oven. Break chocolate into squares and put into plastic bag. Place on a solid surface.

2 With a rolling pin, break the chocolate into chunks. Keep your fingers out of the way!

3 In a bowl, *beat* butter with all the sugar until creamy and smooth. Gradually *beat* in egg.

4 *Beat* in flour, salt, vanilla, and bicarb of soda. Now stir in the chocolate chunks.

5 Spoon mounds onto a baking sheet lined with wax paper. Leave plenty of space around each one.

6 Bake for 10-15 minutes or until golden. Take out of the oven and leave for five minutes to harden, before moving to a wire rack to cool.

Great big chunks of chocolate!

Barbie says:
Try making these cookies with chunks of white or milk chocolate too!

17

Fruity Freezies

Have some of these in the freezer during the hot summer months for a cool after-school treat! They are easy to make but remember they will take a few hours to freeze before you can enjoy them! Creamy Freezies taste great with raspberry or banana yogurt, too. And try Chewy Freezies with pineapple or cranberry juice.

For 2 of each Freezie you will need . . .

For Chewy Freezies

Orange juice

Handful of fruity jelly sweets

For Creamy Freezies

2 small cartons of strawberry yogurt

8 strawberries

Barbie says:
Make pretty Freezies to serve at a party! They are a special treat that can be made well in advance!

Cook's tools

2 plastic cups or yogurt pots

Chopping board

Teaspoon

Sharp knife

2 plastic teaspoons or wooden lolly sticks

Chewy Freezies

1 Line the bottom of each cup with a variety of your favourite colourful fruity jelly sweets.

2 Half-fill with orange juice. Freeze for one hour or until slushy. Stand sticks or spoons in centre.

3 Pop the Freezies back in the freezer for three hours. Remove cups and eat straight away!

Creamy Freezies

1 Slice the strawberries. Layer in cups with the yogurt, tucking some slices down the sides.

2 Freeze for one hour or until slushy. Stand the sticks or spoons in the centre. Freeze again.

3 The Freezies should be frozen after three hours. Remove cups and eat before they melt!

They're so Cool!

Lemon Cooler and Super Shakes

Here are two great ideas for sophisticated drinks. Lemon Cooler is delicious when you're really thirsty, while a Super Shake is rich and smooth, perfect for more dreamy-creamy days. Dilute the Lemon Cooler before you drink it, but gulp your shake straight up and straight away!

You will need . . .

For Lemon Cooler:

Zest of 1 lemon

350 mls/ ½ pint water

Juice of 8 lemons

350 g/14 oz granulated sugar

Barbie says:
For lemon zest, grate just the coloured part of the skin on the finest part of a grater.

For 1 Super Shake:

1 tablespoon vanilla ice cream

150 mls/ ¼ pint milk

3 tablespoons natural yogurt

1 tablespoon honey

For a blueberry shake add:

75 g/3 oz blueberries

For a banana shake add:

1 ripe banana, cut into chunks

For a chocolate shake add:

1 heaped tablespoon drinking chocolate

Cook's tools

For the Lemon Cooler:

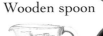

Wooden spoon

Airtight jug or jar

Grater

Measuring jug

Large saucepan

For a Super Shake:

Table knife

A tall glass

Blender

For the Lemon Cooler:

1 Put sugar, water, and lemon zest into a large saucepan. Stir over a low heat until sugar has melted.

2 Turn up heat and bring to a *boil*. Stir for five minutes then remove from heat and let it cool.

3 When mixture is almost cold, add the lemon juice, pour into an airtight container, and chill.

For a Super Shake:

1 Put banana, blueberries, or drinking chocolate into blender with other ingredients and *blend* until smooth.

Pour Lemon Cooler over ice and dilute (approx 1 part Cooler to 5 parts water)

For an extra cool treat, put your glass in the freezer for ten minutes before pouring in the shake!

Blueberry Super Shake

Rainbow Snack Sticks

You can make a Snack Stick with anything that will fix on a stick! Try crunchy vegetables, tasty fruit, or even chewy sweet treats! They look so pretty and the tasty dips make them even more tempting. Let your friends choose their favourite things to eat, and make their own colourful Snack Stick!

You could use . . .

Basil leaves

Cheddar cheese

Asparagus, cooked

Peppers

Cherry tomatoes

Pepperoni slices

Prawns, cooked

Mini hot dogs or sliced large ones

Mozzarella cheese

Olives, stoned

Mango

Strawberries

Marshmallows

Chewy sweets

Fudge

Banana

Chunks of melon

Cook's tools

Chopping board

Wooden skewers

Sharp knife

Tablespoon

Small mixing bowl

Cookie cutters

For the sweet dip:

1 tablespoon icing sugar

200 g/8 oz cream cheese

Handful of mini marshmallows

Juice of 1 orange

For the savoury dip:

2 slices of bacon, grilled and crumbled

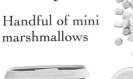
2 tablespoons mayonnaise

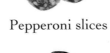
1 tablespoon sour cream

1 tomato, seeded and *chopped*

1 Choose foods that will look and taste good together. Then cut them into chunks or shapes.

2 Now thread everything onto skewers. Combine them in a way that shows off colours and textures.

3 Make dip by mixing either all the savoury ingredients together or all the sweet ones.

Looks like fun!

Try this for delicious savoury dipping!

These bite-sized hot dogs taste great with crunchy pepper strips

This pretty dip is as sweet as you!

Use cookie cutters to make great shapes from mozzarella cheese

Make a traffic light stick from three types of melon

For a very special snack, try prawn, asparagus, and mango

Barbie says:
Skewers are sharp. It's best to take your snacks off their sticks before you eat them!

Cute Cookies

Aren't these the prettiest cookies you've ever seen? They are perfect for a party and lots of fun to make. I have made a bouquet of flowers, but you could use any shaped cookie cutters. Decorating them is the best part — invite some friends round to help!

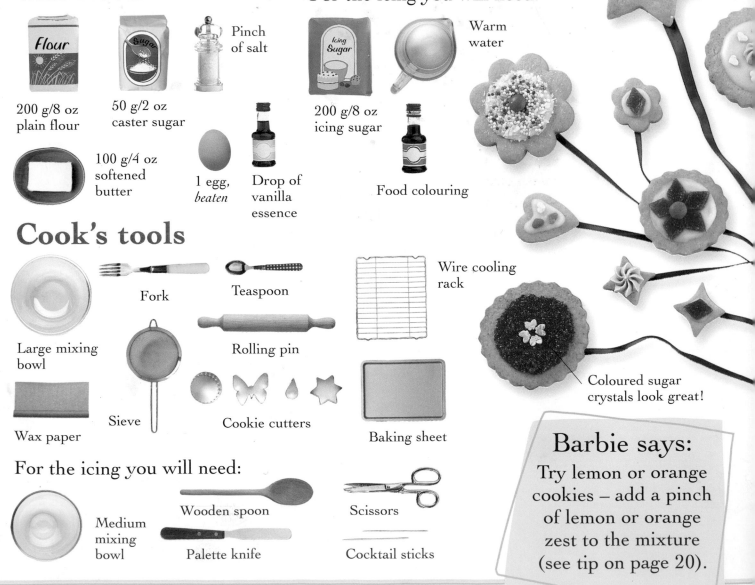

Use a palette knife to spread the icing

To make about 20 cookies you will need . . .

200 g/8 oz plain flour

50 g/2 oz caster sugar

Pinch of salt

100 g/4 oz softened butter

1 egg, *beaten*

Drop of vanilla essence

For the icing you will need:

200 g/8 oz icing sugar

Warm water

Food colouring

Cook's tools

Fork

Teaspoon

Wire cooling rack

Large mixing bowl

Rolling pin

Wax paper

Sieve

Cookie cutters

Baking sheet

For the icing you will need:

Medium mixing bowl

Wooden spoon

Scissors

Palette knife

Cocktail sticks

Coloured sugar crystals look great!

Barbie says:

Try lemon or orange cookies – add a pinch of lemon or orange zest to the mixture (see tip on page 20).

1 Preheat the oven. *Sift* flour into a bowl. Add butter and *rub in* flour until mixture looks like fine breadcrumbs.

2 Stir in the caster sugar. Add the egg, a little at a time, stirring with a fork until the mixture sticks together.

3 Gather the mixture together and place on a floured surface. Sprinkle a little flour onto your rolling pin, too.

Use sweets or coloured sprinkles as decorations.

4 Roll out to 5 mm/¼ inch thick and cut out shapes. Transfer to a baking sheet lined with wax paper.

5 Bake for 20-25 minutes. Remove from oven and, after five minutes, move to a wire rack until cold.

You could arrange green ribbon between your cookies to make a bouquet

Now make the icing...

Oh, so pretty!

1 *Sift* the icing sugar into a bowl. Stir in water, a little at a time, to make a thick paste.

2 Add drops of food colouring, using a cocktail stick, until you have just the right colour.

Beautiful Birthday Cake

Birthdays are a time for parties, and this is the perfect cake for a celebration! Icing and decorating it is lots of fun — let your imagination run free! Your cake will look so pretty you won't want to eat it, but luckily it tastes just as good as it looks!

You will need . . .

For the cake:

150 g/6 oz softened butter or margarine

3 tablespoons strawberry or raspberry jam

3 drops vanilla essence

150 g/6 oz self raising flour, *sifted*

150 g/6 oz caster sugar

2 tablespoons warm water

1 teaspoon baking powder

3 eggs, *beaten*

A little oil for greasing

For the icing:

150 g/6 oz icing sugar, *sifted*

Red food colouring

Warm water

To decorate:

Coloured sprinkles

Sweets

Cook's tools

Sieve

Large mixing bowl

Small mixing bowl

Wax paper

Wooden spoon

Brush

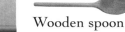
Wire cooling rack

Tablespoon

Scissors

2 x 18cm/7 inch loose bottomed sandwich tins

Palette knife

Pencil

Barbie says:

If the cake mixture is too thick at stage 3, add a teaspoon of water and beat again.

1 Preheat oven. Grease tins. Use the base of one tin to draw two circles on wax paper. Cut out and place one in each tin.

2 Put all the cake ingredients (except the jam) in a large mixing bowl. *Beat* well with a wooden spoon.

3 When your mixture drops easily from the spoon, put half in the bottom of each tin. Level out the mixture.

4 Bake for 25 minutes or until cakes feel firm in the centre and are golden brown.

5 Cool for five minutes, then slide knife around edges and move cakes to wire rack. Remove paper.

Birthday girl!

You can buy icing in tubes to make flowers

Use a palette knife to spread the icing

You could colour ready-made icing and cut out shapes with cookie cutters

6 In a small bowl, stir jam to soften. When the cakes are cold, spread half on bottom of each.

Now make the icing on page 24 and decorate your cake.

Sweet Dreams

You and your friends can have so much fun making these delicious treats! Nuts and fruit are good for you — and they taste great. For something extra-special, why not try dipping little cookies or marshmallows into creamy white chocolate? Arrange your Sweet Dreams beautifully, so they look just as dreamy as they taste!

You could use . . .

100 g/4 oz good quality chocolate

Dried apricots

Cherries

Strawberries

Little cookies

Marshmallows

Chopped nuts

Brazil nuts

Coloured sprinkles

Cook's tools

Wax paper

Large heatproof bowl

Scissors

Baking sheet

Small saucepan

Wooden spoon

Barbie says:
For melted chocolate that is smooth and shiny, keep the heat low and try not to stir!

As sweet as you are!

1 Break the chocolate into the heatproof bowl. Small chunks will melt more easily.

2 Rest the bowl on top of a pan of *simmering* water (don't let it actually touch the water).

3 When the chocolate has melted, take the bowl off the heat, and stir gently once or twice.

4 Dip fruit, nuts, etc., halfway into chocolate and then into chopped nuts or sprinkles.

5 Lay Sweet Dreams on a baking sheet lined with wax paper. Leave to set in a cool place – but not the fridge – for an hour before taking off the wax paper and serving.

Wrap your Sweet Dreams in pretty paper and give them away as presents

Pick-up Pizzas

Everybody loves pizza! There are so many different toppings to try, and I love to test out new flavours on my friends. For a special occasion it's fun to make lots of different ones — they look so colourful and taste just great!

For 10 you will need . . .

For the base:

½ teaspoon mustard

½ teaspoon baking powder

½ teaspoon paprika

¼ teaspoon salt

100 g/4 oz self raising flour

25 g/1 oz Cheddar cheese, grated

1 egg, *beaten*

25 g/1 oz softened butter

1 tablespoon milk

For the tomato sauce:

12 g/½ oz butter

½ teaspoon caster sugar

½ an onion, *chopped* finely

½ a 400g/14oz tin *chopped* tomatoes

1 teaspoon tomato purée

Ideas for toppings:

Mozzarella cheese

Peppers, sliced

Olives, sliced

Mushrooms, sliced

Pepperoni slices

Sweetcorn

Asparagus, cooked

Red onion slices

Pineapple chunks

Ham, sliced

75 g/3 oz Cheddar cheese, grated

Cook's tools

Grater

Large mixing bowl

Wax paper

Wooden spoon

Baking sheet

Saucepan

Rolling pin

Teaspoon

Palette knife

Fork

Chopping board

Scissors

Sharp knife

1 Preheat the oven. Put the base ingredients in a bowl and *beat* well to form a dough.

2 Place dough on a floured surface. Divide into ten pieces. Roll each into a ball, then flatten.

Now make the tomato sauce:

3 Place rounds on a baking sheet lined with wax paper. Prick each base with a fork.

4 Melt butter in a pan and cook onions until soft. Add all the other ingredients and *simmer*.

5 When the sauce has thickened, after about ten minutes, spread a little on each base.

Now put the pizzas together:

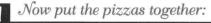

6 Now lay on your choice of toppings, sprinkle on the cheese, and bake for 20 minutes until golden and bubbling.

Say "cheese"!

Don't spread topping right to the edge of your pizza base. If you leave a little gap they are easier to pick up!

Barbie says:
Use cookie cutters to make shapes from cheese and ham, then decorate your pizzas!

Burger Bites

These burgers are best! With this recipe you can make eight mini burgers or four big burgers for really hungry family and friends! Try serving them in ciabatta rolls or pitta pockets for a change, with a crunchy green salad. Don't forget the ketchup!

You will need . . .

4 or 8 burger buns, dinner rolls, or pitta pockets

450 g/1 lb lean minced beef

Black pepper

½ teaspoon salt

1 egg yolk

½ teaspoon mustard

½ teaspoon Worcestershire Sauce

½ an onion

50 g/2 oz fresh breadcrumbs

1 Peel the onion and *chop* finely using a sharp knife. Transfer to a large mixing bowl.

Serve your burgers with any of the following to make them extra tasty:

Mayonnaise

Tomato ketchup

Slices of cheese

Lettuce leaves

Slices of cucumber

Slices of tomato

Red onion rings

2 Add minced beef, egg yolk, breadcrumbs, mustard, Worcester sauce, salt, and pepper. Mix well.

Cook's tools

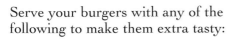

Chopping board

Large mixing bowl

Sharp knife

Fork

Palette knife

3 Heat up grill. Divide mixture into either four or eight. Roll into balls and flatten with a fork.

4 Carefully lift your burgers onto the grill pan with a palette knife or fish slice.

5 Cook each side for five to ten minutes, or until firm and brown. Larger burgers will take longer.

Burgers are brilliant!

You could serve homemade salsa with your burgers (see page 40)

For a spicy burger, stir a few drops of chilli sauce into mayonnaise or ketchup

Barbie says:
No buns? Try shaping the mixture into sausage shapes around wooden skewers and grilling.

Dippy Chicken

Here's a fun and different way to eat chicken that the whole family will love, and there's a tasty peanut dip to serve, too! In the summer, cook these on the barbecue for that extra special chargrilled flavour!

For 12 you will need . . .

For the marinade:

| 3 chicken breasts | 1 tablespoon soy sauce | 2 tablespoons clear honey | 1 teaspoon mustard | 1 tablespoon natural yogurt |

For the peanut dip:

2 tablespoons peanut butter

2 tablespoons soft brown sugar

1 tablespoon soy sauce

2 tablespoons warm water

Barbie says:
Soak wooden skewers in water for an hour before using them to keep them from burning on the grill.

Cook's tools

Small saucepan

 Tablespoon

 Wooden skewers

 Chopping board

Sharp knife

Wooden spoon

Large mixing bowl

Lip Lickin' Chicken!

Serve your peanut dip in a pretty dish or saucer

1 Using a sharp knife, carefully cut each chicken breast into four strips lengthwise (or more if they are large).

2 Measure the marinade ingredients into a large bowl and mix together well using a metal spoon.

3 Drop the chicken into the marinade and stir until each piece is well coated. Cover and refrigerate for one hour.

For a tangier taste, try adding a little garlic, ginger or chilli to the peanut dip!

4 Preheat grill. Thread chicken loosely onto skewers. Grill for five minutes, turning once. Discard the marinade.

5 Now make the peanut sauce. Put all the ingredients in a pan over a low heat. Stir until well-mixed and warm.

Wooden skewers are sharp – always slide your Dippy Chicken off the skewer before you eat it.

Perfect Pasta!

Do you have a passion for pasta? Try my two favourite sauces — Tangy Tomato and Perfect Pesto. They're easy to make, delicious to eat, and look so sophisticated!

For 4 people you will need . . .

1 teaspoon olive oil

1 teaspoon salt

250 g/10 oz spaghetti or pasta shapes

For Perfect Pesto Sauce:

2 cloves garlic, peeled and crushed

50 g/2 oz Parmesan cheese, finely grated

50 g/2 oz fresh basil leaves

3 tablespoons pine nuts

100 ml/ 4 fl oz olive oil

To cook pasta or spaghetti:

1 *Boil* a large pan of water. Add salt and olive oil. Drop in pasta (if using spaghetti, push down with a spoon until it softens).

2 Cook according to instructions on the packet, then taste a piece to see if it is done. Strain through a colander.

For Tangy Tomato Sauce:

1 carrot, *chopped*

1 stick celery, *chopped*

400 g/14 oz tin of tomatoes

3 tablespoons tomato purée

1 clove garlic, peeled and crushed

150 ml/ ¼ pint water

Salt and pepper

1 onion, *chopped*

1 tablespoon olive oil

Cook's tools

Blender

Measuring jug

Saucepan

Tablespoon

Wooden spoon

Garlic crusher

Grater

Colander

Sharp knife

Chopping board

For Perfect Pesto Sauce:

1 Put the crushed garlic, basil leaves, pine nuts, and grated Parmesan cheese into a blender.

2 *Blend* until smooth, pouring the oil in gradually as you go.

Pretty Pasta Colours!

Mix the pesto into pasta just before serving

For Tangy Tomato Sauce:

1 Heat the olive oil in a pan. Add onion, garlic, carrot, and celery. Cook for five minutes or until soft.

2 Add tomatoes, purée, and water. *Simmer* for about 45 minutes, stirring every now and again.

Spaghetti or other ribbon pasta works well with either of the sauces

Barbie says:
To make your tomato sauce even more tasty you could add olives, capers, pepperoni, or a little chilli sauce.

3 By now the sauce should be thick. Taste and add a little salt and pepper if you like.

37

Jazzy Jackets

Here's how to make an easy and delicious meal out of a potato! Baking them takes a long time so you'll have plenty of time to choose which tasty filling to put inside. Jacket potatoes are good for you, too, but try to eat all the crunchy skin and don't add too much butter!

For 3 jackets you will need . . .

3 large potatoes

1 tablespoon olive oil

Salt

Cook's tools

Small mixing bowl

Sharp knife

Baking pan

Fork

Tablespoon

Chopping board

For Cheesy Bean Filling you will need (per potato):

3 tablespoons baked beans, heated

2 tablespoons Cheddar cheese, grated

A few drops of Worcestershire or chilli sauce

Salt and pepper

Sprinkle extra cheese on top!

Cheesy Bean Filling

For Tasty Tuna Filling you will need (per potato):

2 tablespoons tinned tuna fish

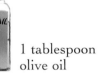
1 tablespoon sweetcorn

1 tablespoon mayonnaise

Salt and pepper

For Pepper Punch Crunch Filling you will need (per potato):

3 tablespoons cottage cheese

Salt and pepper

1 tablespoon raisins

½ a green and red pepper, *chopped* small

1 Preheat the oven. Wash potatoes under running water. With a fork, prick each one several times.

2 Roll potatoes in olive oil in a baking tin. Sprinkle with salt and bake for 1 – 1½ hours.

3 Now make the filling. Simply mix all the ingredients together in a bowl and season. Chill.

Barbie says:
Take care when eating your Jazzy Jacket. It's going to be Hot-Hot-Hot!

4 After one hour, test your potatoes. A sharp knife should slide in easily if they are done.

5 Using a sharp knife, make a cross in the top of each potato, and spoon in your filling!

For a special treat, put a little butter into your potato before the filling!

Pepper Punch Crunch Filling

Which is your favourite filling?

Tasty Tuna Filling

39

Nacho Nibbles

Having a sleepover is lots of fun, especially with a plate of Nacho Nibbles to share. There are so many things you can add to the recipe; they will taste deliciously different each time you make them — the only problem will be making enough for everyone!

For 2 to 4 people you will need . . .

2 tablespoons Cheddar cheese, grated

Large bag of tortilla chips

For the salsa:

1 small red onion, *chopped* finely

½ a 400 g/ 14 oz tin tomatoes, sieved and *chopped*

1 teaspoon caster sugar

Salt and pepper

Pinch of chilli powder (optional)

You could add any of the following toppings if you like:

Pepperoni slices

Olive slices

Pieces of green pepper

Cook's tools

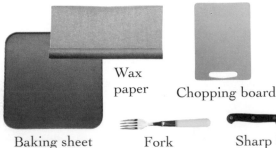

Tablespoon

Wax paper

Chopping board

Small mixing bowl

Grater

Baking sheet

Fork

Sharp knife

Scissors

Teaspoon

First make the salsa:

Now put everything together:

1 Preheat the oven. Put the tomatoes in a small bowl. Add the chopped onion and mix well.

2 Stir in the sugar, salt, pepper, and chilli (if using). Mix everything together well and taste.

3 Now empty the bag of tortilla chips onto a baking sheet lined with wax paper and spread out.

It's **fun** to **Share!**

Barbie says:
You could serve your Nacho Nibbles with side dishes of guacamole or sour cream!

4 Spoon tomato salsa over chips, followed by any extra toppings you want to use.

5 Sprinkle the cheese on top and put in oven for five minutes, or until cheese has just melted.

Don't leave your Nacho Nibbles in the oven for too long or they will be too hot to eat!

41

Super Sundaes

The cool thing about sundaes is that you can make them with almost anything that's sweet and delicious. Surprise your friends with a sundae of their favourite fruits, cookies, or ice cream. Here are two great combinations for you to try. Which one do you like best?

A crisp wafer fan makes a classy addition to any sundae.

For a Fruity Sundae you will need . . .

 2 tablespoons raspberries or strawberries

 2 tablespoons *chopped* pineapple

 2 tablespoons blueberries

 ½ a kiwi fruit, sliced

 2 tablespoons vanilla yogurt

 2 scoops strawberry or raspberry ice cream

 Coloured sprinkles

For a Chocolate Sundae you will need . . .

 2 scoops chocolate ice cream

2 tablespoons mini marshmallows

 1 small banana, sliced

 Handful of mini cookies, or broken up big ones

1 tablespoon plain chocolate, grated

1 tablespoon toffee sauce

Cook's tools

Sharp knife

Tablespoon

 Chopping board

Sundae glass

Ice cream scoop

42

I wish it was sundae every day!

This pink icing flower makes my Fruity Sundae even more tempting.

1 First prepare your ingredients, then layer them in a pretty glass.

2 For a striking sundae, separate different colours and textures.

3 Top with a layer of ice cream or yogurt and decorate as beautifully as you can. Eat straight away!

A pretty glass is essential for a stylish sundae!

Barbie says:
Spoon some whipped cream on the top of your sundae for an extra special treat!

Best-ever Brownies

Here's a great idea for a sleepover treat! Brownies are easy to make and are delicious as a bedtime snack, with a glass of milk or juice. You could try adding pecans or walnuts instead of almonds — and white chocolate brownies taste really yummy, too. One is never enough!

To make about 15 brownies you will need . . .

100 g/4 oz butter

2 eggs, *beaten*

200 g/8 oz soft light brown sugar

50 g/2 oz good quality dark chocolate

 1 teaspoon baking powder

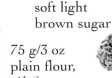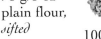 75 g/3 oz plain flour, *sifted*

 100 g/4 oz *chopped* almonds

Pinch of salt

Cook's tools

Medium saucepan

Wire cooling rack

Large heatproof bowl

Palette knife

Fork

Small mixing bowl

Sieve

25 x 15 cm (10 x 6 inch) shallow rectangular cake tin

Wooden spoon

Pencil

Wax paper

1 Preheat oven. Grease tin well. Draw around base on wax paper. Cut out and place in bottom of tin.

2 Break chocolate into heatproof bowl and melt with butter over a pan of *simmering* water.

3 Take bowl off the heat and add all the other ingredients. *Beat* well with a wooden spoon.

4 Pour the mixture into the lined cake tin and bake for 30 minutes or until firm to the touch.

5 Let brownies cool in tin before cutting into squares and transferring to a wire rack until cold.

Barbie says: When you are melting the chocolate, try not to let the bowl touch the *simmering* water!

Brownies before bed!

Two Minute Treats!

These are the perfect treats if you are in a hurry, or are just so hungry you can't wait to dig into something delicious! Each recipe takes just a few minutes to prepare and even less time to eat!

Munch Mix

The perfect, healthy snack – great after school or while watching TV! Mix together two tablespoons of at least three of the following: nuts, sunflower seeds, raisins, dried fruit, or coconut.

Banana Booster Energy Sandwich

Feeling tired? Try this! Spread a piece of brown bread with peanut butter and top with a sliced banana and another slice of bread.

Salad Snack Stop

Try this pretty mixture of flavours for a healthy snack! Combine shavings of Swiss cheese with seedless grapes, nuts, celery, and salad leaves.

Popcorn Perfection

For a sweet sensation, melt a tablespoon of maple syrup and pour it over a bowl of popped corn. Sprinkle with a little cinnamon and eat straight away, while it's still warm!

Ants on a Log

How's this for a creamy crunch with punch! Cut a piece of celery into 2 inch/5 cm pieces. Fill hollow with cream cheese and sprinkle with raisins.

Fruity Floaters

For a delicious snack, make some pretty Fruity Floaters and sail away! Cut an apple into eight pieces and remove the core. Make triangles from cheese and fix them to the apple with cocktail sticks!

Dreamy Creams

Make hot chocolate according to packet instructions. Top with hot frothy milk (use an electric hand mixer), or whipped cream, grated chocolate, and marshmallows. Dreamy Creams taste great with chopped nuts and ice cream too!

Fruit Fantasy

To make four Fruit Fantasies, *blend* or use a fork to combine 250 g/10 oz raspberries, one teaspoon lemon juice, 25 g/1 oz caster sugar, 150 ml/¼ pint double cream, and 125 g/5 oz fromage frais. Decorate and serve. Blackberry or Strawberry Fantasies taste great, too!

A Delicious Dip

Serve warm tortilla chips or colourful, crunchy vegetables with this: Mix three tablespoons sour cream with two tablespoons grated cheese and one tablespoon salsa (homemade, page 40, or from a jar). You could add lots of things to the sour cream and cheese mixture instead of salsa. Try a tablespoon of pesto (homemade, page 36, or from a jar) for a pretty, herby green dip.

Barbie's Picture Helper

Sometimes recipes contain words or instructions that you might not understand. I hope this picture guide will help you with some of them.

Blending Mixing ingredients together in a blender or liquidiser until smooth. Don't overfill the jug; always make sure the lid is on firmly, and ask an adult to help you!

Chopping Cutting into small pieces. For onions, peel and cut in half widthways. With the flat side down, make cuts through onion. Now turn and make more cuts at right angles.

Rubbing in Mixing butter or margarine into flour using just your fingertips (the coolest part of your hands) until the mixture looks like fine breadcrumbs.

Boiling Cooking something in water that is boiling (bubbling fiercely). **Simmering** Cooking something liquid over a low heat so it is bubbling gently, but not boiling.

Beating Stirring something really hard until it is smooth. Beat cake or biscuit mixture with a wooden spoon and beat eggs with a fork.

Sifting Shaking flour or icing sugar through a sieve to get rid of lumps and make it light and airy. Use a wooden spoon to help you.